The Gospel

A Modern Bible Commentary

BookCaps Study Guides

(An Imprint of Golgotha Press)

www.bookcaps.com

Table of Contents:

About BookCaps Bible Commentaries

BookCaps Bible Commentaries are non-denomination study guides for people who are just getting into the Bible for the first time, or who just want to know a little more.

Each commentary, looks at the historical context behind the book, the themes, who wrote them., and study questions. A chapter summary of each chapter of the book is also included.

To find out more about this series and other BookCaps books, visit: BookCaps.com.

Introductions

The book of Matthew is a believer's first written connection with the coming of Jesus and what is known as the gospel story. This book allows mankind to begin an experience of oneness with God that no other religion enjoys. The final chapter in the lives of all believers was set in motion by the penning of this opening book of the New Testament, as it is through the life, death, and resurrection of Jesus that man is able to experience the true love of God. As a believer, sit back now and enjoy a comforting stroll through the book of Matthew.

The Author of the Book of Matthew

The authorship of a book from the antiquities of man is a hard thing to determine and impossible to prove. Many people believe that the book of Matthew was written by Matthew, one of the twelve disciples who followed the teachings of Jesus, the one known as the Messiah to Protestant believers today. When looking at the book, there is not anything that would indicate that Matthew was the author.

Matthew 9:9 allows one to believe that a third person was involved in the writing of Matthew because as it indicates that Matthew was called by Jesus to be his disciple. The language of the scripture indicates that someone else is telling the story and not Matthew.

The book was probably written in the early Hebrew of the time and later translated into Greek. The disciple Matthew is also thought to be Levi, son of Alpheus. He was a Jew and appeared to have the office of a tax collector under the Romans. The fact that Matthew worked for the Romans allows one to infer some information that is not readily available.

According to traditional Roman methods of selecting those who could work for Rome, it can be assumed that he was able to read and write as he would be the one responsible for keeping records and writing reports to the Romans. He was apparently a citizen of Galilee but nothing is known about the city or tribe of Israel to which he belonged. As a tax collector, the Romans would have to have implicit trust in his honesty. Trust was not normally extended to the normal Jew of the day. It is very possible that Matthew was able to communicate in Hebrew as well as Greek, which would indicate a certain standing in the community.

Something must have impressed Matthew in the invitation that Jesus extended to him as he willingly left a profitable life to become a servant. We know that Jesus then went to Matthew's house and was there entertained and met other tax collectors; he also met the rest of Matthew's family. This meeting also allowed Matthew's family to hear Jesus speak.

After making his decision to follow Jesus, he became committed to Jesus and the word that he was bringing to the people. After the death and ascension of Jesus, Matthew remained in Jerusalem and received the Holy Spirit along with the rest of the disciples.

Matthew continued to teach in Jerusalem and developed a following. It is not known where, when, or how he died, but it is doubtful that he suffered martyrdom as this is not mentioned in the other three gospels. For someone as important as Matthew, the fact remains that Matthew is only mentioned four times in the rest of the New Testament. Again, as you prepare to walk through the book of Matthew, realize that there is not a way to know who wrote the gospel of Matthew and to worry about that fact would not be a good use of time. One of his followers probably wrote the book of Matthew from the teachings he received from Matthew.

Bible scholars tend to place the date of the book from AD 60-65. Who wrote the book is not as important as what the book has to say to the people of the world, then and now.

Historical Background of Matthew

Matthew is not the best history book ever written. What Matthew is concerned with is not this world but the next. There are things that happened in the world that were never written in Matthew because they were not important to the overall purpose of Matthew. With that being said, what a student needs to concentrate upon is the scriptures as they will relate to a believer, today.

Some things written in Matthew cannot be substantiated in what recorded history there is of the time. Did these events happen or are they just a story that was told around a campfire late of the evening?

The student of Matthew should relate to these stories only as they impact the material being studied. As the book of Matthew is being read, realize that the book was written by a Jew for the Jews of the day. Common acceptance of the time Matthew was written falls between 60 and 65 AD.

The thing that is important in the study of Matthew is the condition of the people in the study. What was their world like? What was life like for the common man of the day? The reality of Herod the Great is a part of history and can be found in the major history books of today. His family was in control of a major portion of the Middle East at the time Jesus was born and then for many years after the resurrection of Jesus and his ascension.

Modern archaeology has documented the existence of many places mentioned in Matthew. The excavations of Caesarea Maritima and the Roman Jericho show that Herod and Pontius Pilate were real as many inscriptions bearing their names have been uncovered.

The Roman Jericho and Jerusalem were thriving cities at the time of Jesus and Matthew. As one visits modern Jerusalem, reminders of the time of Jesus are found everywhere. The Mount of Olives is still there as is the village of Bethany. Excavations on the south of the Temple have uncovered the steps that led up to the original Temple, possibly the very steps that Jesus walked and taught from. At the north end of the city there are two excavated pools that are considered the Pools of Bethesda where the lame man was healed. On the south end of the Old City are the remains of the Essene Gate and near this gate is the house of Caiaphas the high priest who questioned Jesus.

One of the most powerful finds of recent times is the bones of a crucified man named Johanan. The bones have nail marks in the wrists and in the heel bones. This man died in the same manner as did Jesus. Considerable thought can be given to the economic conditions of the common people. Those who owned land were generally farmers who were able to grow enough for the family. The surplus could be sold to the merchants of the cities.

The hard currency could then be spent for needed supplies and livestock. It would be easy to consider these people as third world people, but they were not. They generally had a comfortable lifestyle and as long as the crops made, they would have money with which to pay the necessary Roman taxes. The people who lived near the lakes and rivers were more often than not, fishermen who also made a good living.

Those who lived in the cities were artisans, storekeepers, and hired helpers. Another part of the economy was the Roman soldiers living in the cities. They spent their wages at the shops and thus contributed to a ready cash flow in the local economy. Traders also flourished in the area and were serviced by caravans that plied the country bringing in goods to be either sold or traded. Everything was not all calm in the land of the Jews. The people hated the fact that they were under the rule of the Romans, and the Roman tax hand fell heavily upon them.

There was constant talk about a revolt against the Romans, but every time the Romans got news of an uprising, they would strike first and very brutally against those whom they thought were leading the revolt. The Zealots often bore the brunt of Rome's tough rule. The Jews felt that God would one day send the Messiah to them; they also believed the Messiah would lead them out of Roman captivity. They were really expecting a military leader to defeat the Romans and reestablish Israel in all of its glory, but such was not to happen.

The Purpose of the Book

Every story must have a beginning. Little Red Riding Hood and Gone With the Wind start somewhere and at some particular time and then the story is unfolded for the reader. The Bible is the same way. The first three books of the New Testament are called synoptic gospels.

They are very much alike in their content, wording, and writing style. Matthew, Mark, Luke, and John all bring to believers the story of Jesus. John takes a slightly different perspective of the life of Jesus. The books are not really biographies but rather are theological writings. Matthew was written primarily to the Jews. The book of Mark was written to the believers in Rome.

Luke was dedicated to gentile believers wherever they might be located. John is different in that it is written to new believers and unbelievers. The book of Matthew is written in such a way as to prove that Jesus was the Messiah. For their entire life, each Jew knew that the Messiah would come.

The expressed purpose of the Messiah would be the deliverance of the Jews from the Romans and the establishment of a kingdom on Earth. The Messiah would rule over the entire world with justice and he would be a descendent of the House of David; this was proven through the genealogy presented in Matthew. It is not hard to understand why the Jewish leaders would not accept Jesus as the Messiah. Jesus, in their eyes, was certainly not a warrior king. Matthew, in writing to the Jews, sought to prove that Jesus was the Messiah.

The Jews overlooked the prophecies of the Old Testament and never took into consideration that a new kingdom could be established on earth without the need for war as witnessed by the conversion of Matthew. The new kingdom would be predicated on service to others and the teaching of how to love one another.

The authority of Jesus is presented by Matthew in the reporting of the miracles of healing, casting out of demons, and raising the dead. When Jesus knew that his time was near spent, Matthew brings forward the teachings of Jesus about what the future would be like and how to live until that future is realized. Matthew presents to all believers that Jesus is the way that believers can establish a relationship with the living God and be secure in the fact that one day all believers will be with God in paradise.

The book of Mark is written by a follower but not one of the twelve. It apparently was his goal to bring the good news to the people of Rome, the seat of civilization. He does this by revealing who Jesus was through the miracles he performed, not just through his words.

The miracles that the people witnessed were important in securing the identity of Jesus. It is thought that Mark was in the Garden when Jesus was arrested and taken before the Jews; he fled as he was about to be arrested. Mark ended up in Rome as he felt threatened by the Jews in Jerusalem.

The teachings of Jesus were important in the story that Mark would lay out for all to see, again the coming of the kingdom on Earth, in a place that was ripe to hear the gospel, Rome. Luke was probably the best educated of all the writers. He was a Greek, a gentile, and a doctor.

The story of Luke is the only gospel that was written by a gentile. Luke also wrote the books of Acts. Paul was a special friend of Luke and no doubt had a considerable influence in the writing of Luke. The book has been called the most comprehensive of all the gospels and stresses the relationships that Jesus had with people. Prayer, angels, and miracles fill the book and give believers a special feeling about themselves. Women are also given important shrift in this book.

The last gospel is a bit unique in that it establishes the fact that Jesus was with God at the beginning. The book was written by John the apostle and brother of James. For all intent, the book was written to new believers and those who did not believe. John reports on six miracles that are not included in the other gospels, again to prove the authority of Jesus over this world. John puts much emphasis on the fact that Jesus came to the earth in a form that man could understand.

In this form, people would have a reference point to consider when making their profession of faith, later. The deity of Jesus is discussed in every chapter of John. Remembering that every story must have a beginning, it is a good idea to realize that the believer has four beginnings with which to contend. Now is the time to look at the first beginning, the book of Matthew. (Life Application Bible p1938, p2042, p2112, p2212.)

Writing Structure of the Gospels

One of the most difficult things to do is to look at a sample of writing and try to tell who wrote it or even when it was written. The four gospels, Matthew, Mark, Luke, and John are an interesting study in writing style and what were important to each writer.

The gospels are the story of the mortal life of Jesus, the one the believers called, the Messiah. Looking at each book, there are some things that might be said about the writing style, author, and purpose of the book, but one might wonder why this is of any importance to a believer.

The stories in Matthew, Mark, Luke, and John are not about the daily life of Jesus. The books do tell us who Jesus was. They also go into great detail about what he did and what he said. Matthew, Mark, and Luke are a collection of very similar facts and utilize common wording of the time, but the books do not all contain the same information nor always agree on chronological order.

The Gospel of Matthew is the only that book of Matthew records the visit of the wise men and the star in the east. Jesus is mentioned as being a carpenter only in the book of Mark. The visit of the shepherds to the manger is recorded only in Luke and John is the only gospel that mentions that Jesus turned the water into wine. In and of itself, these facts are inconsequential because what the story of Jesus is all about is the establishment of a relationship with God.

The main points of the books are all the same yet they are a bit different because in that each person is writing from a particular point of view. Matthew was written to convince the people of the divinity of Jesus as the Messiah. Matthew did his best to inform the Jews that this was the Messiah the Son of David. Mark is a bit different because he was appealing to the gentiles--those not of Jewish heritage. Mark was more interested in what Jesus was doing than what he was saying.

The cultural explanations that he presents were necessary to the gentiles as they did not understand the Jewish faith. Luke represents the most educated look at what Jesus was doing. Luke was a Greek and thus a gentile. As a doctor, Luke had more education than any of the other writers of the gospels and he wrote in Greek. His presentation is very polished and literary in every sense of the word. Women are very important in the story he presents.

The gospel of John is considerably different from the other three. The vocabulary, phraseology, and presentations of the events are vastly different from the other three gospels. John's main purpose in writing his gospel was to stress the fact that Jesus is the son of God and thus was divine in the flesh. Also interesting about John is that no mention is made of the fact that Jesus had a forty day experience in the wilderness nor does the book mention the casting out of evil spirits.

Themes of Matthew

Jesus Changes the World

The entire world was changed with the coming of one man. Never would the world be the same for anyone who accepted his leadership. God's chosen people were in a sad state at the birth of Jesus.

The priests had been praying for the coming of one they called the Messiah and whose coming would signify the ending of all Jewish suffering and subjugation. The shackles of serfdom would be flung off in one glorious move, and the enemies of the Jews would be put on the run.

The Messiah came, but they did not recognize him. When Jesus started teaching, people started to listen and began to follow his leadership. One man! One world! One big change!

Angelic Communications with Mankind

Angelic Communications with MankindSince the beginning of time man has had the ability to communicate with angels and with God. In the Old Testament, there are many instances where either God or an angel communicated with man.

As the New Testament is opened to all believers, again man is being talked to by the angels. The first conversation in the New Testament was the angel telling Mary what to expect. Mary ended up changing the life of Joseph because the angel then went to Joseph and communicated with him.

An angel communicated with the wise men of the East and sent them home via a different route. Again Joseph was touched by an angel, and he took his family and fled to Egypt. All believers can relate stories about being touched by an angel at some moment in their life (Bible, Matthew 1 &2).

The Effect of John the Baptist

The Effect of John the BaptistThe story of John the Baptist is a story in and of itself, but as Matthew is considered, believers need to know that John was to prepare the people for the coming of the Messiah. No doubt he was a strange looking man, dressed as he was, but God uses all people in whatever state they may be found. He was a voice crying out in the wilderness warning people to confess their sins to God and to repent of their evil ways. In his own way, he had his followers or disciples, and he also had a great number of enemies, including the priests. (Bible, Matthew 3)

Baptism with the Holy Spirit and Fire

John told the people that the one following him is much greater. He mentioned that he baptized with water alone, but the one coming after will baptize with the Holy Ghost and fire.

Not commonly known, but the Jews also believed in a Holy Spirit, but they did not know what it really was. Some scholars would have believers to think that John was looking ahead to what he would not know as Pentecost. John wanted people to know that he was not worthy to even hold the sandals of this individual who was to come (Bible, Matthew 3:11).

Temptation can be Overcome

After Jesus was baptized by John, the Spirit then led him into the wilderness where the devil would tempt him. He fasted for forty days and nights and the devil then came to him. The devil then tried to get Jesus to prove he was the son of God by making the stones into bread, and Jesus responded that bread alone is not what makes a man live. The devil then took Jesus to the highest point of the Temple and tempted him to throw himself down so that God would save him. Jesus responded that it was not right to tempt the Lord. In one last attempt, the devil took Jesus to the top of the tallest mountain and told him that he would give all that was before him to Jesus if he would but worship him. Jesus reminded him that man should worship only the Lord and only serve the Lord. The devil left Jesus and angels came and ministered to Jesus (Bible, Matthew 4:11)

The Development of Faith in What Cannot be Seen

Faith is the essence of things believed without the comfort of having seen them. When the next breath is taken, it is taken because until now every time a breath was needed, it was there. Faith is demonstrated by the fishermen who left their nets to follow a stranger. (Bible, Matthew 4:18).

The Roman Centurion demonstrated faith as he asked Jesus to heal his servant without having to go to the centurion's home. (Bible, Matthew 8:5). The leper came to Jesus and exclaimed that he knew that if Jesus were willing he would be healed (Bible, Matthew 8:2). The woman who had been bleeding for twelve years knew if she only touched the robe, she would be healed (Bible, Matthew 9:20).

The Kingdom of Heaven

The first time that Jesus mentioned the kingdom of heaven was in Matthew 5:3.This is part of what is referred to as the Sermon on the Mount or the Beatitudes. When one looks at the entire sermon, the thought must come to mind that this is what must be done in order to inherit the kingdom.

Another name for this would be a code of ethics or a standard for living life for God. As one studies the Sermon on the Mount, he is forced to realize that a man could not possibly follow all of the laws and be sinless. In Matthew 7:13 believers are admonished that the only way to enter heaven is through the narrow gate. Taking this into consideration how can man enter the kingdom? Jesus answers this question in Matthew 19:26 where he reminds his disciples that with God, all things are possible.

Miracles are Real

It has been said by certain scholars that the age of miracles has passed, but when pressed about their statement, they have no defense. Miracles are real. The Bible is full of miracles, and they were reported by more than one writer. Many of the miracles that believers hold to are the ones where people are healed. The feeding of the multitudes always draws a considerable amount of attention as well. Miracles are a bit more restricted in the world of today, but when you hear stories of a life being saved that in reality is a miracle.

Those Who are Blessed

Again the believer is drawn back to the Sermon on the Mount as that is where one will find the characteristics of those who are blessed. Matthew 5:1-12 lays out what God expects of his followers. The Lord favors those who mourn and are meek. He also looks with pleasure on those who hunger and thirst for righteousness and are merciful to those around them. If one is pure in heart and seeks to be a peacemaker, he is a son of God. Those who are persecuted because of what they believe will inherit the kingdom of heaven. When the believers are persecuted for all manner of things concerning God, they will receive their reward in heaven.

The Importance of Being an Example to Others

There is many little sayings that should impact believers in the most powerful manner. "Preach the gospel every day. Use words only when necessary." (unknown) "There are times when the only Bible a person will read is you." (unknown) As people grow up and mature, looking back on life one is able to see that a certain individual had an impact on the way life played out. In many instances, this person would have been a father, mother, uncle, or a friend.

Teachers, preachers, firemen, and policemen will also find their way into that listing. Somewhere one might find a Sunday school teacher or a youth counselor in the mix. What must be realized by each believer is the fact that people judge the effectiveness of religion by what they see in a believer's life. Jesus lived his life to demonstrate how people are to act in any given situation.

Sin Must be put out of a Believer's Life

John the Baptist came to the people extolling them to put their sinful life behind them. He used Isaiah 40:3 in encouraging people to walk as the Lord requires. The Bible is full of prophets who admonished the people to stop sinning and trust the Lord, but Jesus went one step further. He let people know that a good tree bears good fruit and not bad (Matthew 7:18). This was his way of telling people that in order to get to heaven, sin cannot be part of an individual's life.

Vows and Their Importance

Vows were important to the people living at the time of Jesus. They appeared to verify the truthfulness of a statement or an agreement. In our courts, we place our hands on the Bible and vow to tell the truth.

In the eyes of Jesus, this should never be necessary because we are bound by God to tell the truth all the time. Yes should be yes and no should be no (Matthew 5:37), and to say more would be from the devil. The sad thing about the world today is the fact that sometimes we are forced to be less than truthful because of our humanity. When the wife asks if the dress makes her look fat, what will be your answer?

Believers Must Serve Others

Even the disciples were not free from the desire to be served. Jesus had been teaching that it is better to serve than be the master. In Matthew 20:20, the story is told of the mother of Zebedee's sons asking Jesus for special treatment of her sons.

Jesus reminded her that that decision was not his to make as God decides the greatness of a man. Through his discourse, Jesus taught that the greatest in the kingdom of God is really the servant of all. The servant who serves others before himself finds great favor in the eyes of God.

How One Achieves Heaven

Again, believers are called back to Matthew 5:3-11 where what is good is laid out for all to see. Being about these things one will find favor in the eyes of God and heaven will be theirs. Believers must also keep a pure heart and not lust after the things of this world.

They must not seek revenge over a perceived wrong that is done. Straight is the way and very narrow is the gate that leads to salvation and few will enter therein. When the disciples complained about it being so hard to attain heaven, Jesus reminded them that with God nothing is impossible.

Watching for the Final Judgment

Always important to the disciples and the believers was the concept of the final judgment or the return of Jesus to the world. Jesus reminds the believers that only God knows when Jesus will return to the earth, and Jesus does not even know the timing.

Matthew 24:4 reminds the disciples that they must be on guard against false prophets who would claim to be him. What believers call the Rapture is mentioned in the reading and describes two men working in the field, one will be taken and one will be left. Following this logic two cars could be going down the street, one driver would be taken and the other would continue. One could imagine the results of the Rapture.

Chapter Summaries

Chapter 1

The genealogy of an individual fixed his status in the world. It was evidently Matthew's purpose to prove that Jesus was the Messiah as promised in the Old Testament.

The Messiah was to be descended from the house of David and born to a virgin who had never known a man. The first miracle about the birth of Jesus was the fact that Joseph was to be his earthly father, a just man. He did not want to hurt Mary in any way. When the angel appeared to him in his sleep, there was no question about what he would do.

Discussion Questions

Why was Matthew so intent on providing the genealogy of Jesus?

What does the first chapter of Matthew tell believers about Joseph?

Give some thought to the existence of Angels.

Chapter 2

The arrival of the Magi from the east bothered Herod. He was afraid that he was going to lose his power as the king. It was his idea from the beginning to kill the baby who would be a king.

The Magi was instructed in a dream to return to their homeland by a different route. Joseph was warned to take Jesus and Mary to Egypt. Herod became enraged and had all of the baby boys, two years and under, slain. An angel appeared to Joseph, after Herod had died, and told him to return to his home. They made their home in Nazareth and Jesus became known as a Nazarene.

Discussion Questions

The story of the Magi is probably one of the best remembered parts of the Christmas story, for several reasons.

Where do the Magi fit into your understanding of the Christmas story?

For a second time, the angel of the Lord appeared to Joseph with special instructions for the little family. Explain the importance of these instructions.

The slaughter of the innocents is the term given for what Herod did to the male children, two years of age and under, in Bethlehem. This event cannot be proven or disproved. What does that do in your mind about the truth of the Bible?

Chapter 3

John the Baptist is presented in this chapter. He was preaching repentance as the kingdom of heaven was near. He must have made quite a sight dressed as he was and eating locusts and wild honey. Yet a following developed around him and he had disciples who traveled with him. John baptized people with water and told of one who was coming who would baptize with the Holy Spirit and fire. Jesus appeared to John and was baptized. When Jesus came out of the water, the heaven was opened, a dove descended to his shoulder, and a voice said, "This is my beloved son in whom I am well pleased."(Matthew 3:17)

Discussion Questions

The prophet Isaiah spoke of someone coming from the wilderness who would be preaching repentance from the sins of mankind. This prophet would be telling people that the Kingdom of heaven was very close. Would you have listened to such a man?

Repentance is something that all believers must do. Explain repentance in a form that you will remember.

John baptized Jesus. Explain what super natural event happened at the time Jesus came out of the water.

Chapter 4

Jesus is now led into the desert by the Spirit to be tempted by the devil. Jesus fasted forty days and nights before the devil came to him. The devil tempted Jesus to turn the stones into bread, and the devil was reminded that man needs more than bread to live.

The devil then took Jesus to the top of the Temple and told him to throw himself down to the ground, if he were the Son of God. Jesus reminded the devil that a person does not tempt God. The devil took Jesus to the top of a mountain and was told that all would be his if he would but worship the devil. Jesus reminded him that only God was to be worshiped. The devil left Jesus and the angels came to minister unto him. Jesus then went to Capernaum and began his ministry. While in Galilee he called his first four disciples, Peter, Andrew, James, and John, all fishermen. Jesus began healing the sick and preaching the good news to all who would listen.

Discussion Questions

If a person has never had the opportunity to disobey, what could be said about his obedience?

Jesus was in the wilderness for forty days before the devil approached him. The devil, Satan, had to know that Jesus was the Son of God. As Jesus was fully man, what should his physical condition be after forty days?

Being fully man, consider the temptation that could have been felt by Jesus as the devil approached him. Is man tempted more today?

What is the relationship between temptation and sin? If one is tempted, has he sinned?

What makes mankind so vulnerable in the world of today?

How does mankind test God, daily?

The first four disciples chosen by Jesus were fishermen. Is that fact significant for any reason?

When you observe something that appears to be magic, what do you think of what was observed? If someone were sick and you knew that he was sick, and suddenly he was made well, how would that impact your thinking?

We know nothing of the education of Jesus. How do you account for his tremendous knowledge of the Law and life in general?

Define and compare spiritual sickness and physical sickness.

Chapter 5

Near Capernaum, Jesus delivered the Sermon on the Mount which some called the Beatitudes. He stressed that position, money, and authority were not important to him.

What Jesus stressed was faithful obedience and how people should live. The Beatitudes are really what God expects of the people who would follow him. What is stressed in the Sermon on the Mount is a way of living that will be rewarded in heaven.

The parables are also started in Chapter 5 where he reminded the people that they are the salt of the earth who needs to let their light shine out so that men may witness their good works. Jesus taught about how bad anger is and to stay away from lusting after the flesh. He stated his position on divorce and the importance of keeping vows. Jesus ended chapter 5 by reminding people that they must love their enemies.

Discussion Questions

The Sermon on the Mount is also known as the Beatitudes. How are the Beatitudes a (1) code of conduct, (2) an expression of what God values, (3) a demonstration of real faith, as opposed to superficial faith, and (4) fulfillment of the Law?

Salt offers flavor to food. Believers are similar to salt. Explain what you might see as the relationship between salt and believers.

What might the responsibility of a believer be in relationship to the rest of the world, during his life?

Anger is the fire that makes the pot boil. According to Matthew 5:21-26, what is expected of a believer? How does anger relate to retaliation?

Probably when describing "lust" one would need to think about the sexual act between a man and a woman, but there is much more to "lust" than that. Divorce and the breaking of vows are also part of the consequences of being lustful. Lusting after the "good" things of life might just heap on individuals exactly what they are not searching for.

Chapter 6

Jesus was very concerned about those in need. He mentioned that when helping the needy not to make a show of doing it. Jesus wanted people to know that God knows what they need, and he will respond to the supplications of his people. He reminded the people that they should never make long rambling prayers to get each other's attention.

God wants a believer to pray in a closet with the door closed. Forgiveness is also stressed in this chapter as is the proper use of money. When fasting it is good that nobody knows that you are fasting. Jesus also stresses that worry is a waste of time and that a believer should be concerned with seeking the kingdom of God.

Discussion Questions

Living the life that Jesus taught the believers would make the world much more user friendly. How do you view the needy of our world and our ability to help improve their lot in life?

It has been said by many scholars that if you can talk, you can pray. Jesus demonstrated throughout his life that prayer is an important concept that must be followed by his followers. What do you consider when you pray to God?

Along with prayer is the practice of fasting. How are fasting and praying related to the lifestyle of man, today? When praying what is the believer really looking for?

Chapter 7

Judging or being critical of others is not a proper thing to do. Believers should be seeking the kingdom rather than belittling a neighbor. The Lord knows what one needs and will provide for those who are seeking him. God expects all believers to treat each other in the manner that they would like to be treated.

In his teachings, Jesus reminds the people that the narrow gate is what must be passed through in order to get to heaven and that people will be aware of one who is not of God. By doing the will of the father, those who believe will find their way to heaven. In doing the will of God, man is building his house on the rock and not the shifting sand.

Chapter 8

Jesus is about healing in this chapter. He heals a man with Leprosy. The man demonstrated great faith in the ability of Jesus to heal him. Another demonstration of faith was the Roman Centurion.

The Centurion's servant was ill and needed healing. Jesus was willing to go the Roman's house, but the Centurion confessed that Jesus could do it from where he was--an example of great faith. He healed Peter's Mother-in-Law.

Jesus healed a young man who was taken over by demons by sending them into a herd of pigs. Jesus demonstrated his power over the storm on the lake by calming the bad weather.

Discussion Questions

Decide what the term "faith" really means to you as an individual. To follow the teachings of Jesus, believers must really trust and have whatever "faith" really is.

Explain to yourself why one would sometimes have to see in order to believe?

In your view, what does the calling of Matthew really demonstrate to the world?

Chapter 9

Chapter 9 brings the first confrontation with the established church. When Jesus healed the paralyzed man, he said, "Son, be of good cheer; thy sins be forgiven thee" (Matthew 9:2).

The Jewish teachers thought that he was blaspheming! Knowing what the leaders were thinking, he made sure that they knew he considered himself the Son of God and able to forgive sins on earth. It was at this time that he called Matthew into his service and went to his home to eat with other tax collectors and Matthew's family. Jesus spoke with such authority that one lady, who had been bleeding for twelve years, knew that all she had to do to be healed was touch his robe.

Chapter 10

At this point in the book of Matthew, Jesus prepares the twelve disciples to go out and get some experience in the country. He made sure that they knew they would be harassed, but he reminded them that they could endure. Jesus gave the twelve the power to heal, raise the dead, and the ability to drive out evil demons.

The disciples were to depend upon God for their leadership and to not even take any money with them. Jesus reminded the disciples that whoever would not accept them, they were to move on to another place.

Discussion Questions

Jesus sent his disciples out in the country about them and gave them authority to accomplish many great things themselves. Why?

When a believer considers the world about him, at what particular time will his work be completed?

Chapter 11

As strong as John the Baptist was and in spite of what he saw and heard when he baptized Jesus, he still had questions. He sent his disciples after Jesus asking if he was the Messiah or should another be expected.

Jesus answered by having John's disciples report back to John what they had seen. Jesus praised John for being such a servant for God, but the lowest raking angel in heaven was ranked higher than John. Jesus extends the call to all who would follow him in Matthew 11:28 when he speaks about his yoke being easy and the burden being light.

Discussion Questions

When considering the Kingdom of God, there is a particular way in which one will move towards being part of that Kingdom. In your own words how does one become a part of the Kingdom of God?

Chapter 12

The Jewish priests were very legalistic and tried to stick to the law as they understood it. By doing this, they were putting an excessive burden on the backs of the people. The disciples had just walked through a wheat field and gathered some heads to eat, which according to the Jews was doing work on the Sabbath. To further enrage the priests, Jesus healed a man's hand on the Sabbath.

As the crowds increased around Jesus, the priests became worried about his influence and started talking against him and saying that he was under the power of the devil. The Jewish leaders wanted to see some sign that he was really the Son of God.

Discussion Questions

Think about the Sabbath Day and determine if the day belongs to man or God.It has been said that a house divided against itself will not be able to stand, yet it also appears that Jesus was doing just that to the Jews in Matthew. How could two Jewish peoples exist?

Chapter 13

The parable of the four soils is explained in Chapter 13. In reading what is reported, a believer can hold to the truth that there are a variety of believers. Some believers will produce more than others, but this shall not be held against all who strive for the Lord. It is all up to the follower of the Lord to make the most out of what is given him. Persecution will come to all who wait on the Lord and those who are weak will fall away from the Lord.

Discussion Questions

Give some thought to the possibility of different levels of belief among the community of believers.

Chapter 14

Chapter 14 brings some sad news to Jesus in the form of John the Baptist being killed by Herod. A big question was raised in the mind of Herod as he thought that Jesus was John the Baptist, raised from the dead to continue his attack on Herod.

Upon hearing the news of John's death, Jesus wanted to withdraw to a quiet place, but the crowd continued to follow him. It was now time to eat and Jesus had the disciples to sit the people on the grass, and with five loaves and two fish, he fed 5,000 people.

Discussion Questions

Upon seeing Jesus walking on the water, Peter asked the Lord to allow him to walk on the water to the Lord. Jesus bid him to come to him on the water. How do you account for what happened next?

Chapter 15

Inner purity was very important to Jesus. The Jewish elders wondered why the disciples did not wash their hands before eating as it broke the Law. Jesus took this opportunity to teach people about being clean on the inside. He reminded them that what went into the mouth did not make a person unclean but what comes out of the mouth may condemn a man forever. Evil thoughts come from the heart and are expressed through the mouth. Eating with hands that are not washed is not what makes a person unclean.

Discussion Questions

The purity of man is more than a physical thing of washing one's hands and eating only clean food. Jesus expanded the Law by doing what?

Chapter 16

The Jews were always asking for some sign that they could then believe. Jesus told them that by looking for a sign, they were testing God and he left them without any type of sign. He told them that they could read the weather, but not understand what they were seeing. Jesus took this opportunity to warn his followers against the wrong teachings of the Pharisees and Sadducees.

Jesus inquired of his disciples about who he is in the eyes of the people. He then asks Peter about his thoughts and Peter confessed that Jesus was the Messiah and Son of the living God. Jesus admonished his disciples not to tell anyone who he was, and it was here that he first predicted his death.

Discussion Questions

When teaching the scriptures to believers and unbelievers, it is important for the teacher to teach true to the word of God. What did Jesus find disconcerting about the teachings of the Pharisees and Sadducees?

There is one denomination that considers itself to be the Church of Saint Peter. In your mind's eye, why is this important?

Jesus predicts, for the first time, his coming death and will do so twice more in the balance of Matthew. Accepting this prediction is an important part of the faith that a believer must have, why?

Chapter 17

At this point things really began to change for the disciples. Heaven was proven to Peter, James, and John as they witnessed the transfiguration and Jesus told them not to tell anyone what they had seen until after he was resurrected from the dead. After healing a demon-possessed boy, Jesus witnessed about his coming death, for the second time.

A temple tax was due at Capernaum. Jesus sent Peter fishing and told him that there would be coin in the mouth of the fish. It was with that coin that the tax was paid.

Discussion Questions

Of what importance is the Transfiguration, in your own words?

The responsibility of being good citizens falls heavily upon a believer's shoulders. Regardless of how one considers his situation, believers are foreigners on this earth because a believer's true home is with God. How do you practice good citizenship?

Chapter 18

If one is looking for angels among the disciples, none will be found as they are still human and they were worried about who is greatest in the kingdom of heaven. Jesus reminded them that all must become as small children, and humble themselves in order to enter heaven.

Temptation still found a home among the disciples and Jesus warned against that. He warned them to never look down on any individual lest they commit a sinful act. Forgiveness is tied into how believers treat each other. God will forgive as others are forgiven.

Discussion Questions

The world causes problems for many people. Believers, just like unbelievers, are always in a struggle seeking an identity for themselves. The mistake with that tact is, if allowed to mature, that positions of importance will be sought. Who will be the most important person in our little group?

How can one prevent oneself from falling into that temptation?

Chapter 19

Jesus now has the undivided attention of the Jewish leaders. They see him as a threat to their leadership, and for sure, they did not want to share authority with Jesus. Many people were now following Jesus. Marriage and divorce again entered the picture, and Jesus explained his position on the subject. Again he blessed the little children and reminded the people that the kingdom of heaven belongs to such as these. When the people heard these things, they were sure that nobody could enter heaven, and here Jesus reminded the people that nothing was impossible with God.

Discussion Questions

Give thought and voice to the proposition that all must become as little children to enter the Kingdom of God. Gaining admittance to the Kingdom of God is not the easiest of tasks. Giving thought to how bad life is on earth how can one expect to make it to Heaven?

Chapter 20

Chapter 20 brings to all believers the beautiful story of the first being last and the last being first. The landowner wanted to treat everyone the same. This sounds a bit like God wanting everyone to have the same opportunities.

What makes the story a little sad is the fact that man wants more than he is entitled to. For the third time, Jesus predicts his death and this time the mother of James and John ask that her boys sit at the side of Jesus, one on the left and one on the right. More discussion was had about being first and last.

Discussion Questions

Service is a way of life for the believer. Where can you see yourself as being a servant to those around you and how will you go about becoming a servant?

Chapter 21

This chapter of Matthew allows for Jesus to enter Jerusalem as was predicted, riding on an ass. The people welcomed Jesus and were shouting "Hosanna to the son of David! Blessed is he that cometh in the name of the Lord" (Matthew 21:9).

The city of Jerusalem wondered at who this was, and they were told that it was Jesus of Nazareth. Jesus entered the temple and drove out those who were selling there. The blind and the lame came and were healed. He left the temple and went out to Bethany were they spent the night.

Discussion Questions

It was necessary for Jesus to ride into Jerusalem on an ass. Why?

The parable of the wicked tenants tells believers much about what was going to happen to Jesus. What do you see as being the same in the parable and the life of Jesus?

Chapter 22

The parable of the wedding feast is mentioned in Chapter 22 and reminds all that many are called, but few are chosen. The Jewish leaders tried to trap Jesus with a tax question concerning whether it was right to pay taxes to Caesar or not. Not to be trapped Jesus asked whose image is on the coinage. He ended up say by telling people to give to Caesar what is Caesar's and give to God what is God's. Jesus reminded the people that the greatest commandment is to love God above all else and to love our neighbor as we love ourselves.

Discussion Questions

The parable of the wedding feasts brings to believers a statement in verse 14 that bears much consideration. What do you see as the meaning of the scripture?

Read Matthew 22:41-46. Why could the Jewish leaders not answer the question that Jesus posed?

Chapter 23

Jesus spoke down to the religious leaders of the day. He warned his listeners to not take the rules of man as seriously as they should take the rules of God. He adjured them to not take the best seats at dinner or to thrill at being called Rabbi.

Jesus wanted the religious leaders to be helping people and not causing them problems. In most instances, it is easy to tell someone how to live, but not live that way ourselves thus making themselves hypocritical teachers and not leaders of the people.

Discussion Questions

Jesus really condemned the Pharisees and religious leaders of the Jews. What did he accuse the leaders of violating or not doing?

Chapter 24

Jesus foretells the future as he mentions that not one stone will be left upon another. All will be destroyed. He reminded them that there will be many who will come in the name of Christ, but they are not. Much is presented to cause the early Christians to worry about the future.

There will be wars, earthquakes, and famines, but the time will not be yet. Persecution will be felt by many. All will be able to see the coming of the Son of Man. There will be no doubt when it is time.

Discussion Questions

Jesus told of the end times and his return. What will be happening in the world prior to his return? How will his followers know that he has returned?

Chapter 25

Jesus had two more very important parables to tell his followers concerning the virgins and the talents. Both of these parables were intended to keep the disciples on the right path.

The believers must always be ready to respond to God when the time is right and can't be trying to purchase oil at the last minute. All believers are given something of value to develop, and when it is not developed, they have not done what it is that God wants for them. Do not hold onto the talent as it is meant to be developed. At the time of judgment, God will remember who has worked for him.

Discussion Questions

What might your special gift from God be? Have you ever stopped to consider what you can do better than anything else?

Chapter 26

Jesus now holds the last supper with his disciples and reminds his followers that he will be crucified. Judas was sent forth to do that which he was meant to do. The supper that was delivered to the disciples is what is celebrated today as the "Lord's Supper" and when it is served, it is done in remembrance of Jesus the Son of God.

Jesus reminded the disciples that after his being raised from the dead he will go ahead of them to Galilee. The disciples were taken with him to the garden where Jesus asked that they keep watch with him, and it was here where he was arrested.

Discussion Questions

Do you consider anything as strange that went on at the trial of Jesus before the Jewish leaders?

Chapter 27

As Jesus predicted he was brought before the religious leaders and in effect given a trial. Judas in the meantime tried to return the money to the temple, but was unsuccessful. Jesus was taken to Pilate.

Pilate's wife warned him to have nothing to do with this man. He tried to release him, but the people rose up. Jesus was flogged and turned over to be crucified. The religious leaders made fun of Jesus on the cross. Jesus died on the cross, and at that moment, the temple curtain was torn from top to bottom.

Graves were opened and saints were seen walking about. Joseph of Arimathea came to claim the body to lay it in a tomb. A great stone was placed over the tomb and guarded by soldiers.

Discussion Questions

In reality, how did the Jewish leaders get Jesus out of the picture?

Chapter 28

On the first day of the week, the two women named Mary arrived at the empty tomb. They saw Jesus, and he told them to tell his disciples that he was going before them into Galilee. The next time he saw them he delivered the "Great Commission" to them.

Discussion Questions

As a believer, what makes the resurrection of Jesus the most important thing that happened in the life of Israel?

Suggested Reading

Barbieri, Louis A. Jr. "Matthew" in The Bible Knowledge Commentary: An Exposition of the Scriptures by Dallas Seminary Faculty: New Testament Edition. Edited by John F.

Walvoord and Roy B. Zuck. Wheaton: Victor Books, 1983.

Bauer, David R. The Structure of Matthew's Gospel: A Study in Literary Design. Sheffield: Almond Press, 1988.

Carson, D.A. "Matthew" in The Expositors Bible Commentary. Volume 8. Edited by Frank Gaebelein. Grand Rapids: Zondervan Publishing House, 1984

Morris, Leon. The Gospel According to Matthew. Grand Rapids:William B. Eerdmans Publishing Company, 1992

Online Resources

http://truthsaves.org/outlines/matthew.shtml, April 11, 2011

http://www.bible.org/Matthew, April 11, 2011

**http://www.theology.edu/biblesurvey/matthew.htm
l**, April 11, 2011

References

Bible, (King James). (1945). Cleveland, Ohio: The World Publishing Company. (Original work published 1945).

Life Application Bible. (1995). Wheaton, Illinois: Tyndale House Publishers Inc. (Original work published 1988)

Printed in Great Britain
by Amazon